The Stone Guest

Other Stride books by the same author:

Concentrated Ground: Selected Writings 1980-90

My Kind Of Angel: i.m. William Burroughs
(contributor)

A Curious Architecture: a selection of contemporary prose poems
(contributor)

Ladder To The Next Floor: Stride Magazine 1-33
(contributor)

THE STONE GUEST

M.A. Duxbury-Hibbert

THE STONE GUEST
First edition 1999

ISBN 1 900152 39 8

Cover art by Susan Duxbury-Hibbert
Cover design by Neil Annat

Acknowledgments
Fire, Global Tapestry Journal,
Memes, Ramraid Extraordinaire,
Stride, Terrible Work.

Published by
Stride Publications
11 Sylvan Road, Exeter
Devon EX4 6EW

Contents

'After the apparition of the *Stone Guest*, I had sat down again to the feast!'

– Gerard de Nerval, *Aurelia*

And, furthermore, loving
My bodily emissions,
Recrafted them through bread & wine
Into a body of work...

Raised Eyebrows & Personal Stink

My neighbour told me
He'd dreamt of bushy eyebrows
In the night.This brushed my dream
Which I'd forgotten until then
In which that featural oversight
Likewise crackled. And in his dream
His neighbour from the other side
Appeared. That cracked my dream
A little wider, though achingly
Largely elusive.

This suggests a mounting terrace
Of dreaming, a spillage from head to head
And bed to bed. What did our other neighbour
Dream, higher up the hill, the one
We seldom talk to in waking life? –
That, in itself, another story.

I sense a progression
Of raised eyebrows
Climbing the hill of dreams.

•

The weather stank, but we
Went out with our neighbours
Wading through dishwater air
At the Easter Sunday car boot sale
Aware (as usual) I needed a bath
Swiftly scanning the stalls
Of musty detritus.

Flicked an 'Everyman' Marcus Aurelius:
The passage on the stench of breath
And armpits. Fastidiously set it down
As it was soiled. Bought a history

Of Elizabethan England, & back in the car flipped open
Onto mention of personal stink.

The 'coming in threes' was accomplished
In this dowsing of nostril connections
When our neighbours raised their
Mutual bad breath, & offered us a freshener.
Like poetry, it burns
The tongue in patches,
Heats the mouth. Like
Oxter avidly lapped
Yields stinging salts
And special acids.

Back home, refreshed with connections,
I've still not had my bath (Time being too busy
Weaving these things in its web)
So I carry the essence over
Another day.

Shaken Down In The Red Grove

I.

He bedded a tree, amorously
Encircling its girth, awoke
To ringing in his ears
And delighted in the laying
Down of process. In the soft bed,
Filling out the folds with images
That solidify, limbs which involve
With a gratifying resistance, grafting
Moon-struck bone-beams
In measured morning light.

It began with hidden spirals
Like black smoke in the earth
Which spin from their own involvement
With a terrible effort, an evolutionary
Eccentricity, shifting from the unregenerate
Axis, moving out & up towards expectancy,
Branching complexity in a simple sky
Vast & blank & shafted with eyes
In the beams of which the blind thing stands.

Where they cross, become
Candelabra-branched, the arches & the architraves
Enfold & span & lift
Upon the root.

II.

A crawling thing, something of blood & wine,
Sprawling, needing support, with little purchase
On the earth. A trellis of correspondencies
Might hold it all together, might frame
Its rig of flourishes.

Meanwhile, grove dwindles to vineyard,
Untrained tendrils involve the foot,
Queer the poet's rhythm, vex his pitch.
On this insignificant soil, all that remains
Of the sacred place is etched inside
His flickering lids. Rapid blinks
Envision parallel landscapes,
Lay down between dearth the lines
Which fruit with a dusky gravity
(Which he fondles when the pickers have left)
Testing the swelling distance
Between finger & thumb, pondering distillation
Of the essence of the vine
Shaken down in the red grove.

'Ah,' he says. 'The moment,' he says,
'When the god emerges from the grape.'

The Last Wizard

Sunlight drains from the church's elevation
And shudders down an unfrequented lane
Suddenly essentially English.

He stands on the threshold
Of his rotten shack, beneath rusty corrugations
Grimly impassive in monumental greatcoat.

Eyebrows crackling, he seeps essence
Of old tom-cat, armpit of elderflower
Cradling his retreat.

His pockets bulge with putrid fetishes,
The bones of tiny animals, queer tackle
Of his vocation, of his craft.

It is what can be seen over the dark shoulder
That begins to fascinate, when attention wanders
To the dim interior, beyond the personality.

Within is the magical memory of a house
Where knick-knacks, pots & pans, cracked cups
Join in a fluctuant dance of remembered objects.

This mad jig is brought on by invention, casting back.
He sees it as clearly as he sees the village boys
Scuttling home with fear-flexed anuses

To tell tales to their brawny mams
Of leaping saucepans, balletic colanders, sieves
Shot through with unholy light

Dancing behind the fearsome wizard wise-man.
Last of his line, black pupils projecting
Abysmally backwards, blindly forwards

Into a future which cannot exist without
Some part of him still to observe.
The dance subsides, the things regroup in stasis

And tall tales rise in yeasty kitchens
Where the boys have run to tell
Of otherness, of all hell breaking loose.

The Egg Is Submerged In The Black Milk

The egg is submerged
In the black milk;
I thrash in a nightmare
Of proteins.

With forced appetite
I approach the bubbling cauldron.

If I waited, if I delayed,
If I did not succumb
To this feeble ritual feast;
If I walked off, empty-mouthed,
And let my body direct itself
Eating light & wind
Somewhere outside the enclosure –
What then? What if I
Put everything off
For long enough
To make a difference?
If I stopped munching & mouthing
So that something else could seep in?

The egg is submerged
In the black milk.
Must I thrust my head
Through that stagnant excrement
In the name of mindless nourishment?

The man with no hunger to feed
Has time to digest the world.

Overlooking The Curve

Heavy rain & mist:
Two pints of beer in a coastal pub
Then sitting in the car,
Window open, steamed up,
Overlooking the curve of the harbour
And pondering the robe of flesh,
The fleeting manifestation.

Rain drums the roof of the car,
Words drum, unspoken, the roof of the mouth:
How I think of our secret marriage,
Words I'd blush to utter,
A spirit marriage, yes.

And robes of flesh,
Again, draped on girlish skeletons,
Can never come between, can never touch
This deepening channel
Of intimate connections
Between two fugitive forms
Fleet & strange on the earth.

(Cemaes Bay, 20.3.91)

Ascending The Three Terraces

Ascending, level by luminous level,
The flower-filled terraces, rising above
The gloom of the family on the colourless beach
Where sunlight slides from each surface
Getting no purchase, ripening no peach.

By the second terrace, keenly scaled
With a sense of liberation super-sexual
The blooms get lit from within, their hues
Flooded with 'it-ness', obvious, how they were meant.

So what veil had descended, back there,
Shrouding the earth in a mucal ectoplasm?

In the retinal resolution of the dream
I clambered upwards, breathing the nectar
Of colours that creamed the tongue,
Blood-reverberant, enzyme-flooding,
Bathing the eyes with balm, sinking
Through every level of body, of spirit,
Down to the luminous sediment
Where the richness touches base.

At the third terrace, the blooms
Were fully fervent, pulsating outwards
To meet me from deep centres, wholly alight.
Like seeing through blood, flowing backwards
And forwards, a blessed exchange, a transfusion
Of thusness.

In waking I jerked & broke
The bedside lamp: bolted back
Into body only to shatter light,
Bitterly regretting my return.

Sick Muse

Her head aches, tremendously, a rotten boulder
Nestled in an arm of land
Tattooed with crude insignia:
Poison throbs in her plundered veins.

Gigantically she lies & suffers,
Stinking, spasmodically swilled with grey rinsings
Wrung from a dishwater sky:
Cradling within the stillborn image
Of what she once was, once might have been,
What should have been meant to be –
Which is her art, through bars of corrosion.

In The Old Railway Carriage To A Background Of Runaway Horses' Hooves

Strapped to the machine
In erotic solitude
The lions & philosophers look on.

I'm sure the great anaesthetist approves.

Divested of tapering
Edwardian footwear
Padding the engraved corridors
In a trance of morbid wallpaper,
The vision erect, on tiptoe,
Ready for sudden exposures
The old equipment couldn't capture.

We must be new, psychic photographers
Fixing the spiritual & the pornographic
In dark rooms worthy of the name

We must perfect the morbid gaze
Swimming in emulsion of lucid daze.

Omnivore At The Dinner Table

In this universe, all devours all,
Yawningly omnivorous, a protein chain of
Sustenance stretching back
Through the fleshy links of which
Green surfaces gather water, convert
The sun.

The mother crushes you to her vast breast,
Cries: 'You're so good I could eat you!'
And you almost wish she would,
Bit by succulent bit.

I stroke my cat, & consider
His back has the contour of a chicken
Trussed & roasted, but furred with mould
Which selective scruples render
Inedible, here & now.

Here & now is a considerable luxury
(We tend to forget) bolstered by wealth (relative)
Sentimentality (inbuilt), human ego (which hasn't much
Use for death, unsquaring the meal)
And a touching fastidiousness
In the face of a howling Nature.

I partake, in essence, hungrily, gratefully,
Absorbing many lifetimes, consumed by greed.
I am composed of old sunlight,
The green of long-gone Summers;
I have devoured the metaphor
Of my forefathers, & regurgitated it
Many-fold.

Nibble your stem, peep from beneath
Your limp leaf, take the pulse
With judicious finger – But look at me accusingly
Across the table, & I'll eat your face!
I devour doubt, as well as anything else,
And, in turn, am devoured.

For everything under the sun
Eats everything else.

Sculpture Stalks Off, Stage Left

Still among the women
Frozen in classical attitude
With my well-thumbed book & marker
Throbbing in the forbidden library, locked
In erotic pose.

Every annealing glance
I stored since youth
Trembles down the length
Of the pointing wand.

I knew I'd finally gather them
All in vibrant lines
To kindle & admire.

The eye of my sex
With jewel inlodged
Follows each graceful lineament
Each floating fold
Billowing then settling
Against a naked foot.

See it flex against the floor
As still the women come & go
Their talk hardening to sculpture
From which the chisel skids.

Throwing down the tool, lopping
Off the patrician proboscis,
Shift attitude, begin to dance,
No longer still amongst the women,
Shattering the forms.

In The Plague Village

In the plague village
Contagion is passed by word of mouth
Warm breath on the face
And a fatal hook in the vitals.

In the fever sweat of nightmare
You awake regurgitating the words
Which thread the corpuscles of your blood
And echo in sleep's aching excavations.

In the plague village
There are no crosses on the doors
But scraps of paper inscribed with
Indecipherable obscenities
Stuck down with gobs of chewing-gum
Smelling of bad breath.

In the plague village
The gaga count is high
And the radiation readings
Bounce from the granite walls
In disbelief.

The villagers have inside information
From undisclosed sources
That the mining operation on the mountain
Is a cover for unclear dumping.
They huddle in fluorescent kitchens
Incubating vague details
Fermenting cloudy toxins of their own.

In the plague village
The word was heard
From a third
Who shall be nameless
But never blameless.

In the plague village
The square is a grid
Of criss-cross resentments
You cross at your psychic peril
Smirks & sniggers rippling
In your wake.

If your wake is strong enough
If you can stay awake long enough
You just might cut a swathe
Through the communal grave
Of the plague village
And emerge alive, & kicking.

When you have placed your mind
Beyond the environs of the village
Your memory of it will resemble
A box of old clothes, close-packed,
Moulding & musty, incubating
The fatal virus
Of the village plague.

It's a big village, now,
To place your mind outside of.

Village Midnight

The front of the house opened outwards
Suddenly, & he knew the home-brewed potation
Had turned the trick: the slanted glass
Slurred his head across the fields
As night air hit him.

A sheep grumbled somewhere
Like a drunkard's stomach
And the air was full of earth-scent,
Animal breath, & human absence.
He brushed a Coleridgean 'vastness'
In a dark Romantic sweep
Of quiff uplifted.

The church tower gathered the night
Into its squat particularity, as
The jars of the present were absorbed
Mercifully in the pub's slumbering stones, as
The last unsteadiness wove the hill to silence.

The village sleeps, it sinks
Gratefully through the mead-soaked levels
Of its history, ferments in its ancient must,
Breathing its dreaming essence gently forth.

At last, he draws back from the gazing,
Removes his reflection from the tilted glass,
Turning his hand to the table. Quiet power,
The work is going well: a feeling of
Positive pressure under the hand,
A drawing together of elements
In the charged magnetic field.

After The Exodus

No news from the front, & now it seems
The village has been evacuated,
Which is good: silence spreads like a balm
On the calm air, & emptiness fills
The tractor tracks, the cottages, the vacant shop.

The last shard of gossip sinks
To the earth, begins to become
Archaeology amongst the worms
And broken cups. Our lips curve
In a smile of blank relief.

We always loved the churchyard
With its green perspective, its pools
Of shade & oxygen, its departed voices
Murmuring the language of dream & memory.

Now the sweet revery has overflowed,
Filling every street & passage,
Flooding the square, climbing the hill,
Bringing white wisdom to the schoolroom,
Narcotic bliss to every nook & cranny.

Why only we remain we cannot tell:
The dream elite need no excuses,
Are no longer dependent on the departed
Babel of collaborations, will not regret
The loss of friends & family, or even
The precious few who spoke our language.

For the longest time we let our tongues
Hang still, & meditate on the motionless clapper
In the church bell, the clock with one hand
Seized in the sleeping tower.

Clare's Trip

Five days
After the storm
On the journey home
From High Beech
Crisp clutch
Of leaves
In my mouth

Spitting
Into the wind
I could see them
Laid out
Before me
A legend
Of my journey

A generation
Still living
Life through ink

Not many of us left

Dull thunder
Claps

The Outline Of That Old Fatality

I can never come down this lane without
Seeing, again, the corpse of the cat
We saw when this walk was new, a lifetime ago:
Soggy black & white, & flat – the memory
In fatal outline, slowly deliquescing.

The image of that death dissolves, into an
Early Spring: gorse, blue air, & novel walks
On which I made the place fulfil
My book-fed inklings of an English lane,
Though this was Wales, & sparser than my vision.

Wherever we walked, we reeled
Our back-projection; our feet
Moved up & down, but our frames were static.
A vital aspect of movement remained elusive,
Somewhere other & else & made
Our gestures stilted, unconvincing, strange.

We used the wrong language, clearly,
Our tongues at odds with the place, the
Taste of foreign air. Novelty can't sustain
A life uprooted.

But who's to talk of roots, when the soil shifts
So relentlessly? Is there a here to perceive
Not steeped in interior culture? Is there a now
We could bear, unshafted by the consciousness
We sink? Is there a reality
Unshadowed by the hidden? – Unavoidable rhetoric,
When asking impossible questions.

Not expecting answers, but riddling the air,
Always the double-walker, at a remove.
The present's never in my stride, that shambles
Shaken down to fit old shadows:
My matrix is the past, & books, & art.

Thrush-song triggers the darkling metaphor
Of all the birds of several English counties;
The churchyard is full of Spencerian corpses,
Big-limbed, square-headed, ready to scramble forth
In my resurrecting mind amongst the stones.
The old house is a setting for that novel
We once read; & one day must re-read, re-write, re-live,
On our ramble full of imaginary second chances.

'I'm never in the here & now,' I said;
But you'd forgotten I walked beside you,
Beating bounds of reference of your own.

And every time, of all the times we've walked
This way, the outline of that old fatality
Stains the mind's-eye corner,
Flickering, darkly feline, on the verge.

Sexing The Demons

It was the first hot sun
Of Spring, in the new intensity.
I shaded my face with my hand
And my arm ached with writing
And my brain with wanting more.

I needed to walk towards
Another element. This inland lake
Will suit my purpose well.

I have to lean in close
To assuage the ache: the ache
Occasioned by this body
That cannot shift shape, except
By supersensual movement, swift poetic drift –
This meat & gristle & heavy liquids
Processing toxins slowly as it moves
Within the confines of its coarse envelope
On which the sun plays,
Teasingly.

The saint proposed a diet of light,
No solids or earthly fluids: to achieve
A shimmering spiritual slimness
To allow passage between worlds.

Pressing my front to a rustic fence,
Peeling to smoothness under the scab
Of crisply lifting bark: the inside is silver,
Hard & cool to the touch.
This hardness, as the sun prises,
Reassures me much
As rhyme to a wandering mind.

I shift my burden from one thigh
To the next, from lobe to lobe.
My sex, these days, is always almost
A property of mind: my eyes slide to the right
Allowing in a compact visualization.

A small thing, a slight familiar,
Looking up appealingly, though distant & uncoy.
And white in its nakedness in a grubby,
Slightly unwholesome, English way. Real,
In fabulous fact, in its dancerly postures –
First against the fence, exhibiting
Buttocks thrust & heel upturned
Coquettishly behind, moss & grass stains on the sole.
Then leaping up to walk the rustic bar,
Its unremarkable feet in stubby gestures
Near my face: heartbreaking sham
Of clumsy balletics, tremulous, crotch agape.

The pleasant part is the imperfection,
The friendliness, the absence of blunt lust.

It's sweet to solve the riddle
Of the ache, which hexed
So many pastorals of the past:
I've sexed the demons into deeper being
By application, white fatigue, & space.

The Uninvited Guest

Meeting, on dissolution of the envelope,
The internal & external vastness,
I can think these molecules apart,
Can introduce a fart that spites solidity
By a playful release of gas.

I am the dangerous guest
At the dinner party, can blow it all away
In a blast of methane mirth.

And, less slapstick, can do other
Quieter transmogrifications, later, alone
In the secret library, you open
Across a sheen of fragrant desk; or,
Later still, if we're mutually lucky,
In select company on a cool slab
Of terrace.

See how the party falls back
And the only voices now caress
The velvet inner ear?

Let the soft fabrics lock in coming together,
Or fall away to nakedness
Unabashed, for seen from either side.

Shall we conjoin, then,
In breathing our molecules apart? –
Soft & expansive
Beneath this milky moon
Discretely together?

The Sibyl Comes Out

The sibyl smelt of mothballs –
(Boyhood fear & lust
Memories of the dark
Closed places, choking fur,
Incarceration amongst shoes,
Stiff suits, the rasp of tweeds,
The relics of old sports…)

The temple was another enclosed space
With its auntie figure rising
From the shadows, its dim relation looming
Between history & spiritual truth.

These potent females stink
Of otherness, of yawning displacements
Of time, so the fucking of the virgin
Becomes a slow horror of having
A crumbling corpse long-shafted.

I forced myself to listen to her words
Though her breath stank of dead earth.

In my dreams she kept her mouth shut,
Presented a radiant cheek to warm
My hungry sense of self: love kiss
In that lost, oneiric realm.

Breaching the cabinet, loosing
Moth-hoard which flutters to instant dust
In the ruthless afternoon, the sibyl
Steps out with moving lips:
In a twin-set reeking of mothballs
Pours forth pearls.

Task of Angels

Dissolute angel, pumping,
Becoming translucent
With sundry others of his sort
Assembled round his task,
Absorbing the darkness of his thrust,
Transforming it into light:
Then all borne off, & weightless.

The Play's The Thing

After the gabble, off to the left,
After the obscenity on the proscenium, archly
I can tread these boards.

Call it the new reality, beyond
The avant garde, call it
The kitchen sink without the pot
And dirty water.

Strangely drugless, mouthing
This cleansed dialogue, pristine
Projection of a solid text
That somehow stays in the head
Like a page we're relieved to re-read
In a calm aftermath
Of controlled performance.

Not leading, but following, men –
Fondly brushing the chalkmarks,
Finding our place.

The Dead See Scrolls

But don't they, in a sudden unravelling
That sickens & exhilarates at once
With everything falling away?

The antechamber smelt of antiseptics,
Compromise, strained relations
Leaning too close, jollying along
A soul grown weary. If you wish to care,
Consider the centuries, that sickness of time,
Scrolled tight behind these fading lights.

Consider (if you care) the wading
Through scriptural fragments, sandals
Filling with sand & soul with grit,
Not finding it, crossing (in a lifetime)
That desert of scholarship – vast dry tracts –
In the forlorn hope of refurbishing
The forest.

It breathes in the back of the brain,
A shiver of pine like an idea oxygenated,
A sudden deciduous shudder.

In the light of the life of the planet, consider
These modern deserts of invention:
Sahara, Scottish Highland, Yorkshire Moor –
The yawning bleaknesses which match mind-climate
As the wind, harsh dominatrix, whips them clean, –
But only when we've stripped & made them ready.
A steady erosion consumes our path, eats into
Soggy soles. Thus, likewise, a single lifetime.

And the bad breath of death unwinds
Its fuming eschatology – foul cupids
Swelling out to fill the sky.

O & fever & chills & heartburn –
My mother scrolled up before me
From old recordings, bits torn away,
By memory abused, showing her capacity
For screaming life & death.

This command of evil, life
In reverse, death on rewind,
Causes us to gibber prayers in spite:
Let it be
'Forbidden to disturb by night in dreams
Or by day in sleep, the male PRK-demon,
and the female PRK-demon,
Those who breach...'
The precious veil.

Let it be forbidden,
With healthy dread, to weave
Too tight these veils; forbidden,
To resist their loosening.

O fever renewed, & chills, & heartburn,
Screwing these sweated sheets,
Forcing swaddling from one's own body,
O mummy, let it be said
'The male-poisoning demon
And the female-poisoning demon
Is forbidden to enter the body.'

De-magnetized, let it be
A whirling while.

So parchment unscrolls, sifted
By grains, shifted through time
To be rediscovered: & something unclassified
Uncoils from its marl enclosure
To feed the parching sand.

Note: Lines in inverted commas are from
The Dead Sea Scrolls by Eisenman & Wise

After The Journey

Reaching down beneath
The bedclothes, lodging his fingernail
Under the rim, the plate of his heel,
He found himself picking away
(In a rising aroma of grey horn)
Great shards of crumbling hoof.

Only partially did he recall
The past night's journey.

A Music With Interesting Problems

The image, O Lord, came away
In my hand, waltzed away
Over tidemark horizon
As I gaped in a gone-cold bath.

I groped for the slippery grip
Of the firm poetic line
I'd learnt I could raise myself on:
With geriatric fervour grasped the bar,
Spasmed reverberant octaves down its length,
Catching spun glass at the limit.

This is modern music, fluidly slopped,
Stopped in its tracks by a crash
Of broken glass, & randomly redirected:
A music with interesting problems,
Shatteringly beautiful.

I Was Never One

Bleached memories of hippy dawns
In a Norfolk cottage: fruit pie
On offer for breakfast, spirals
Of hair pie between the teeth, Beefheart
Asleep on the turntable. Cut to the pub
And crisps & bitter beer, landlord
In Tattersall check & a foul mood.

Some breakfast.
Some weekend.
Some era.

I was never one
For the endless hippy weekend
Although happy to rewrite the hash
Of Beefheart in my head.

Through The Crack

Through a sudden door
In the suddenly stilled bar;
Through a door, dimly, in the corner
Of the eye, where the lights soften
Almost to blindness, & then blink on
With a Christmas tree effulgence
And a nostril sense of pine, clear
As a rush of memory released.

We seek for the crack of this door
Through many such evenings as this, marooned
In these non-eventful places, full
Of present faces in the empty swell
Of time. We bide; our eyes ride
To the unfocussed corner that may yield
Impossible exits into light
When chronology & architecture give.

There are dead heroes, here,
In this hidden room, & our old selves
In soft mirrors, instantly recognizable.

Veiled with the remnants of old glamours,
Punch-drunk with retrospective flashes,
Leaning into cool tiles & purifying porcelain
We void the nausea of nostalgia
And come out whole & steady-stomached
Into rooms of meat & men.

His Tongue, His Book, His Silence

I.

His tongue purple, his breath
Elderberry dark, metallic,
Through chiming fruits of the forest
He makes his way. Full of juice
As he is, his senses are brittle:
Twig snap can shatter him, explode
His crystal concentration.

This hard light in his brow
Is echoed by the weight of sex
He carries against his thigh, is matched
By the upthrust of earth
Beneath his feet.

Trees shiver like chandeliers
Where the forest deepens; leaves exude
A moist interior cool, moss
Clothes & muffles, stream traces
Silver the centre.

II.

The proximity of the trees
Made him feel full
In the trunk, lung-full
In their breathing shade.

And the notion of sap
In smooth green stems
Swaying in crevices, in secret corners,
Made him aware of his juices.

And the nearness of moving water
Percolating through all his senses
Provided a crystal backdrop
To the motion of his mind.

III.

Gnawed by the weather, his book,
Secreted in musty bole, dusted
With fungus, threaded with worms,
Letting air into the words.

He claps it, triumphant,
To his leather breast, cradles
Its weight to lung-swell, aspirates
Against its sweating boards.

Clawed cover mirrors his breath,
The shape of words much-handled,
Much turned on the furred tongue
Through liquor of nights to limpid dawns.

He loves to let it lie silent, his book:
Old friend, his ancient familiar,
Keeping close its hoard of legends,
Mute pillow beneath his head
Which dreams of words, words, –
Then none:

        Cool rock
        Against his ear.

IV.

By night, owl or bat,
Out of his belfry or barn,
Spanning the dark distances,
Filling the illimitable lung
With cool & moonlit space.

From the window, watching, relish
Graveyard wine, redolent resin
Of last year's dandelions
Coating the tongue with dead-men's tang.

Head lifts, the seed is blown,
Reflection shifts.

The harvesting of this mellow vintage
Involved brown thumbnail, shot sperm
From the pinched stem, much bending
In the shadow of church & yew.
The boys made queer shapes between the stones.

Past midnight, when ferment's over,
Refining itself in savoursome stillness,
I set the glass on the cool sill,
And jettison familiars into flight.

In Search Of Characters

He wanted to receive letters from people
Who could become part of his fiction:
Characters picked out in relief
From the swirl, the swamp. He desired
His book to objectify.

He wanted to receive phone calls
(Though he had no phone, nonetheless
He was a receiver) crackling with
Cryptic dialogue, revealingly referential
To the structures of his sub-plot.

Somehow the two sides could be
Brought together in a secret meeting
On level nine of a multi-storey
Dream park, after slithering negotiations
Of barriers, & ramps, & concrete stanchions.

Here the vital documents could change
Hands: he might brush, in trembling relay,
A palm which had lovingly cradled
Treasures he had known, coinage
Goldenly common.

Is it, then, too much to ask? –
A letter, one letter, perfumed
With recognition; one stinking
Phone call, words heavy on air
But light on ear, because they
Click the cypher: like a spring tripping,
A bulb going on
We see ourselves by.

These fictions
Underscore loneliness
And the heavy-breathing
Partner in this night.

Cat-door claps.
At least he has his
Channels through the dark.

The Fetish Of The Gangster-Poet-Priest

Drugging the stalking gangster in his mind
He muffles the scream of the swinging bulb
With armfuls of shot silk: under full sail
For another billowing night.

Beneath his pillow, the secret weapon:
A worn stiletto that's murdered many floors,
Clicked menace in many a midnight street,
And, emptied, fumed in dawns.

The essence of its interior moulds his dreams:
Pungent depressions pressed by mincing toes,
Circuits of air beneath spanning arch
As another fatal step is broached, heel spiking
Into street plans of stale cities.

Sick gangsters sleep in their shoes:
Loosen ties, maybe belts – never laces.
The barefoot mode's anathema to his kind –
Too vulnerable, surface to surface, curved to the earth.
Better gun-metal bitter on hardened tongue,
Shoe leather masking the street
And staining the sheet. Fucks
With his shoes on, toes clamped,
Spiting orgasm.

'Only spaghetti hangs loose,' he snarls –
Then, winding it tight: 'Not for long.'

The Method Of The Gangster-Poet-Priest

Watch him, he's selective,
He'll take bits of you & use them
In so far as it suits his purpose.

In the gloom of his fascist cabinet,
Picked out by trained lights, the disembodied
Parts are on display.

Once he grasps the fragment that he needs
He's off, conjuring his mythic structures,
Oblivious of the severance in his wake.

Fall beneath his piercing gaze, you're abstracted
On the spot: with his swift perceptive razor
Sliced, cubed, & atomized.

Names escape him: they'd clog his system
With individual claims, they'd bind the parts
Too separately together.

His henchmen are the painters, poets, seers,
And his lair is soundly world-proofed
With their works:

With the tip of a finger he summons
Who he needs. They wait in mute attendance
On his bidding, bound to obedience.

He loves to sit in the midnight calm
When he's put the world to sleep
In his humming mind.

Like a hive his head's alive
With the sweet harvest: from defenceless blossoms
Of life he's sucked his manna.

You're elsewhere, in your own recovery,
Folded in private night, dreams torn with the eyes
That plunged into your essence

And then drew back, began to select,
Erasing the details irrelevant
To his field of focus.

He sits with some part of you
In his lap, stroking with quiet menace
His subjugated pet.

When the breathing becomes more calm & regular
He'll take it & lay it, grimly gentle,
On the open page of his book;

Then, looming in the cunning slant
Of his lights, bring the boards together
With slow force

Leaning on closed volumes with massive hands
Until all breath & movement is resolved
And laid to rest.

The eyes of the gangster, upraised
Like the saint's, roll to repose at last
On the poet's page.

Bad Weather In The World Of Sex

Bad weather in the world of sex
As some go moth-eaten in heavy coats
Spitting thick lies into tissues
Hawking their false notorious past
...And some in next to nothing,
Recklessly unseasonal, all peepholes
                    & snarls through emptiness,
All straphanging strangulated orgasms
As the finger twitches on the button
With millennial urgency, & a butt
Flickers into oblivion around the bend.

This artifice of costume beggars the eye:
Strips hanging, corners caught, much
                        unwinding material
Which fails to resolve itself above the knee.
It can only be for the self, you see,
These days, these latter days: for the self
                                    we put it on
This threadbare adoption, which cannot hope
                                  to keep out
Bad weather in the world of sex.

The Wrong Sort Of Silence

In the cold windy road the husband
Is cleaning the car. In the chill hall
She hovers, duster discarded, fascinated
By the darker strip edging the square
Whose folded geometry should rectify
By rights this teetering house.

Light dies with the season, sucked
From the sports ground by the strain
Of being within the big coat of the commentator.
He squares his shoulders before the lens, before
The mirror, lowers his pitch to the mike's erection.

'What I hate,' she says, 'is the way he tells it
All – nothing left out, nothing left alone.
And me here, longing for silence, if only
The silence of this inner loneliness
Where I fight alone with something less
Than devils. Devils would be something:
Something with rills, frills, red thrills,
Smelling of the swamp, compelling
Devils from that earlier time.
No, though. Something less. Nothing:
Something less than nothing. Fighting
Nothing – Shadow boxing.'

And when she comes indoors
There's a larger silence, that isn't
What she meant, not what she needed.
The quality of this silence, strained,
Surrounded with a greater nothing
Than the ache of activity without.

Behind this silence there's a machine
Humming, something other than the utility
Mechanics of this house, something infernal.
The idea of the knives in the kitchen drawer
Is oddly comforting. Odd, she should think of that
As her eyes glint from the surfaces, the units.

She seems to see endless cold suburbs
Mushrooming over a green dream of some past
Which somehow isn't hers & never was.
She longs to float down this dream
In a bliss of acquiescense, beyond
The vacancy, the wrong sort of silence.

How can silence come to be
So wrong? In the cold hall
The crumpled duster possesses all
The graduated intricacy
The transcendent drapery indirectly lit
Of a gown in a medieval miniature
Mesmeric in its tranced detail
Of tiny jewels & punctilious fretting
(All lovingly-worked shadow, all penumbra)
Her world is dropping back from...

Another Kindling From A Little Death

'Roger died on Sunday.' And so he did:
– 'Fools Die' crowed the distorted friend
Plucking the book from the stall
Then shrinking to cigarette mist
In veiled window (several steps removed
From prophecy) – Waiting for the man who never came
Down that street, that street.

And tomorrow we'll join the perennial procession,
Black figures across a hillside, dazed, wooden,
Falling into line on numb feet, finding
That each death provides another block of vacancy
Towards this wall in the consciousness
That stays our hand from the pen, the page.
Almost. For if only to say he can't
The writer brings pressure of words to bear
On that which is inexpressible, & dumb.

My head today is made of wood:
Black, unreflecting, like the primitive effigy
It used to be fun to be
In the stoned corner, nodding at the fire
Of life the others loved to stoke. –Now
Ashes on the tongue, grey ash
Coating the mask gone stiff
With emotional impotence, the rigor
Of finding no words, or only dead ones.
A veil settles over appearances –
Not a breath to lift its hem of dust.

Another little death, & I exaggerate.
But these are exaggerated times, & I
Who am conscious of things I cannot feel
Must needs be raking these ashes
To summon a kindling wind.

His Country Heart

Tucked deep in the corner, the intimate cleft,
Pondering in the enchanted halfway house:
Scintillating highlights, absorbing shadows, boozily
Steeped in centuries of trance. Curtain stirs
In sun-breeze of gone morning – which he pulls.

His nourishment is drawn from the bottomless well.

The texture of his deep tweed
Becomes meditational: the rich weave
Of autumnal shades in microscopic stubble
Captivates the eye & draws it in
To become part of the thread of the tale
He's spinning from his sleeve, where he wears
His country heart.

'One's retina can be balmed with milk,
With images of a dawn barn,
One's senses swamped with sonorous lowing
As somnolence is released from a crush of straw.'

This man tempers his spirits
With the essence of fields
Reverently digesting
His domain:
Mud-man, moulder
Of dark & glutinous
Images, idols of dung.

He fashions them from shadow,
Forcing out air & light with kneading hands,
Broods density into the rude forms
Investing them, mesmerically, with life.

His elbow draws the liquor from the grain.
He's adjusted some saturation of his cells
To accomodate the elements: his crevice
Grows richly brown, gently seeping
An excremental wealth
Composed of the colours
Nature breaks down to claim.

'Holy manure!' is his clarion call
As he takes on the world & ferments.
And what of the vents
In the back of his coat
A playful wind might lift?

'If you followed it through & went further
Entering into the heart of this country
By the back way of thicket, scrub, & waste,
Where might it lead, the passage through leaf rot & mould?
Lifting the russet curtain, passing
Into the tangled labyrinth,
Weaving its coils & twists, what might we learn
Of the functions of this place
Incubating – secretly – dark earth gods in a corner
Tending us back to the soil?'

Come To A Field That Is Wondrous

'He brings his young to the opening of the field...'
– Robert Duncan

Come to a field that is wondrous, enclosing
The commonplace in full daylight
Which is the light of realized dream.

I work on a technique of broken sleep
And day is the break, the shard
With which I irritate the skin of dreams
Exquisitely.
(Job couldn't
Find better work
Find sweeter occupation)

Now the fragments are less
Regularly aligned, connect
Less evenly, are zig-zag
As skull-seam before the coming togther
That restricts in its cohesion.

'Does not your wondrous field have limits?'
Why, yes, or how else field:
But limits, these, but walls
Of beautiful irregularity
With jagged gaps, dream spaces,
Bites of light.

The Legendary Still

Localize the legendary,
Beat the bounds fantastically
So that tales once more encircle
The rock, the rill, the root.

Abstract the particularities
From all the speedy smoothings
And glib assumptions, the smearing machinations.
Realign the old shapes of the village.

Lost to sight, one can smell, still,
The old orchard, can be drunk, still,
On the lingering essence which hangs
Inbetween in suddenly silent air.

These sites are full
Of buried streams & secret springs –
(The ghosts know them, haunt them,
Still) – & our present joy or gloom
Lies in their courses
Long laid down.

Here the parliament of rats
Assembled, filed cavalierly
In top-turned boots & monumental hats
Along the ancient current.

It only takes one to see them
For the tale to fold them in;
One's enough, wobble-legged, double-visioned,
To fashion the visionary origami tableau
From the black paper of gone nights.

Autist As Artist

Only communicating in code
An autist compiling his catalogue
Of mutated equivalencies of things
Touched with the solitary wand
Ever achingly erect, never softening
Into easy familiarity or belonging,
His mission one of alien intent
Light years, dark years from home.

A fervid aloneness of yearning
Consummation could only sully.

The exhaustion begins to show
In the patterns of the watcher's eye
In the movement of his hand
In the rhythm of his sympathetic rocking.
A minute tremor, now,
In the habits of a lifetime
Lending something quirky to the line
A spasm which becomes a queer distinction.

'We must stick with our muses,' he says,
'Our angels & their agents,
Through the thick obscurities of vision
And the thinnesses of perception,
Faithful through failure & infrequent triumph.
We must stay close, once found;
But all is in the finding,
Without which: mute automatism
In a chamber of clamouring echoes.'

Beautiful Eyes

The old engraving
Of Saint Whoever
With the little arrows
Invading his hood & collar
Becomes recognizable
As parallel affliction:
Just note his smile
Of long suffering
And the grizzled beasts dreaming
Oblivious at his feet.

You hold it together
Despite the shower of little arrows
By bestial attention
To the moment: This is
How beautiful eyes are born –

Creation in a blink.

The Great Release

Having untied the black knot of sex
Let dangle the satin ribbons
Sensually diffuse.

Breathe in light as the walls dissolve
Of De Sade's airless prison. All sweat
Drawn away from the laboured act
The body turns in its own illumination.

Evening Of The Ancestors

He's up, long past his bedtime
Spinning lines to meet the deadline
When all the voices converge
In a sofa-scented evening blur
Of soft sound, & the gone rise up
From their long bed of decayed conversations –
Grandfathers, forgotten uncles, faded family friends –
Fluttering, moth-like, mouthing dust
Round the glazed occasional tables of our past,
Our past repasts.

Hear the burr & buzz
Of those rich voices
Moving in & out of sleep,
Of time.

The Face We Deserve

Under his eyes was etched
A lifetime of sensible indulgence
Having laid down the fat lines
Of poeticized experience
In many an over-ripe place
And flown in the face of fashions
Severally natured, severely sexed.

Did it make him more ugly
Than it possibly could
Being more or less a man
And unholy human?

It was an ugliness the soft
Mornings should teach him
To live with, the afternoons to despair of
And despise, the evenings to dissolve
In further blurrings of the mirror.

Sometimes he staggered home
To discover a face like the surface
Of the moon, more pitted
Than to be pitied: cold
And eternally staring –
The eyes a network
Of dry canals, conveying
No cargo, forever
On hold.

Waking Up In An Unmade Life

As if poems were braille on the tabletop
Punctuated by drinks his finger-endings tapped
Blind rhythms in the wet rings.

As if friends were strangers he hadn't met
Catching moist eyes through the smoke of the room
He let them stand, unmade, like the best of his lines.

Calculating in a corner what the world owed him,
Compounding its crimes with morbid interest, said
In his word-drunk simper:
'But I have a living to unmake'.

Poets have the best idea, he said,
It's just that they spend a lifetime
Putting it into words, then
Taking it out on themselves in spiteful silence.

Birth Of The Green Man

Not orgasm as such, but
This slow release of seed
As light, illuminating
All but everything…

'I dreamt a city uprose
Of green towers, & rising
Brushed the sky with sap,
Drew light into the earth.

'It was a city of emerald
Translucense, a chlorophyll metropolis
Telling a tall story, naturally'

The sap held back,
No fool he, unless
A holy one, restraining
Green light grinningly –
Filtering sun & life itself
Intervening where it would fall
With screech & long aftermath.

He preferred the way
Light shafted through leaves,
And leaving well alone,
A sense of health through veins
Contained. It was a circuit
He would break alone.

From this grew his face,
An intertwining, a grimace.

A Green Flash

Away from home, the familiar
At a distance, the first drowse
In the garden confirms
Guardianship by dream of his open head:
Zoom into the warm cavern
Of his space-shifting yawn.

How the sunlight filters
(In these uneasy years)
Through the structure of the animal
To illuminate this interior redly.

Discovering yourself trouserless
In striped deckchair, in a built-up area,
Shirt tail artfully arrayed
Over the pent-up thrust of retention
Which is like the accumulating hum
Rising from the city, pulsing
Against the folds of heat
The Summer builds to climax.

Those moments in history
The hiss of nature behind them
The hum of things unfolding
Leaves - - - - - - - - abruptly.

In a green flash I realize
The secret of time, which
Has been there all along.

I drop the dates to rot
Like a sweet trail in the ditch
Of delicquescense.

How things soften under
This influence. This
Is her deadly secret
Which a breeze fondles
Between my knees
Of grass.

Marginal Illumination

Across the dark level
Of the games field (a line
Drawn under a chapter
In a life) I can see
The family home
Ablaze with light:
'Soul-flooding' might describe, but
All I say with dream-numbed lips is:
'God, she's got all the lights on;
She'll have the place on fire!'

Thus after half a life
And largely wasted
Mother illuminates
My manuscript.

Sudden Phantom

Sudden phantom, the white went up, winged
From somewhere back there, too swift
To put shape to, luminous
In the evening soft, a chill
From the darkening border.

It put me in mind of my mother
Dead these twenty odd years
Leaping back from the derelict door
Into some secret place we dared to explore
On that shared holiday, long ago,
Called life: instantaneous spectral owl
Slapped into birth from the shadows –
And all we could do, & can,
Is cover our eyes & hope for the best
(Our 'windows of the soul' blacked out
Like those of the ruined house)
Shrieking betimes, of course,
In cacophonous unison.

Should one regret that old curiosity
That starts the spectral owl
From its secret darkness?

As futile to regret the stiffening flesh
As it slides back to the source.

A Mouthful Of Violets

The girl throws down flowers,
Torn petals, ripped by her
Bitten nails, heart-rending
In their abused innocence –
A flutter of flirtation.

Follow me along the upland path
She says, in this careless shower,
This girl who'd heedlessly brush away
The intricate webs that vex her
And just as easily see you off
The cliff, with a mouthful of violets.

My real love is the movement
Of the wind in the grass,
In her hair, leading me
Ever further along the path.

The sweet tingle of straying,
The rising rush in the ears
Of the wind in the grass,
And her, head tossing, always
Ahead, her hair alive like the sea
Coming in & out of focus
In the waves of joy and fatigue.

Waking Up Under Wet Blankets

Sex, too, has been hefted aside
To a position where it is almost
Invisible, stretch how one will.

What arrangement of mirror or lens
Could bring it back into focus?
And what image would be reflected
To inspire the frayed libido? –
Male, female; you, myself?

Or would the glass be empty,
A vacuum of old lust
The eye sucks on hopelessly?

This is the nightmare, waking up
Under wet blankets, feeling the weight
Of old bedding burdened
With centuries of broken sleep
And shattered sex.

In The Shadow of The Blush

the orchard walls
are high
& hard
to climb

under a rushing
leaden sky
they dance
the petrified girls
their feet
rooted in earth

the saint erect
with the blush-rose
at his feet
looks on
from a dangerous distance

Memory Of The Hollow

It should be
an interesting journey
despite the pit stops
the afternoons in the hollow
with a low sun
& a heavy cider

I couldn't get inside her
in the hollow
the day turned
metal-tasting
our lips were coated with it
it killed intercourse
stone dead

It remains
an interesting journey
as I recreate it
tell you of it
remind myself
remind us
of it

Retain the idea
remind yourself
of an interesting journey
tell yourself the story
of that life

Whatever it was
or wasn't
in the hollow
ring of death

Ancient Wisdom

Pythagoras tunes
The first guitar
Fingers
The ancient screw

Fretless mind
Attuned to triangles
The basic magic
Of music & maths

•

Look not
In the mirror
By a source
Of light
Nor attempt
To retrieve
What has fallen

Touch not, especially
The white cock
Nor share thy roof
With migratory birds

•

Acknowledging
Three sides
To every problem
Put wayward fancy
To sleep
In the Pythagorean tent

Dawn kisses
The equal sides
Dew balms
The argument
Falls geometric

Her Movement Undoes

The dancer's bare legs, opening
And closing like scissors:
Hot heels to vulva folded
Then point of strong feet
At full & sinewy stretch.

This action of limbs, of muscle
Drawing the mind; & the face behind
In classical withdrawal
In concentration distanced from the body.

Mind matches the scissor action
Of sundered threads, of beauteous ribbons flying
Her movement undoes.

Significant Soil

Spontaneous resurgence of old grief
Stirs the fur of the first remembered pet.

Such a black hole in the memory –
The plot is lost where the little body was laid.
I cannot return to that garden.

Time turfs it over, it passes
Out of the family, so slight
The tenure, so brittle the scattered heraldry
Of undistinguished bones.

The garden washed by surges
Of nostalgia informing all its colours
Becomes eternal, a forever garden,
A garden of first dawns & last burials.

Who was the man who lowered the little box,
Smelling of shoes or chocolate?
Father? Uncle? Mother's pet? –
Such stark blue eyes of Summer ice
Overwhelming the afternoon.

Strange Sons

Strange sons, unbinding
The specifics of time & birth
In random exploration – Old men
Should be thankful of such.

Suns anticipated by old moonlight
Might never make the sky
Dissipating the dark drizzle
Of history's nostalgic spell.

That we, in that time, could be there:
Back over that hill, those little figures,
The we of us in our dark village.

In the monochrome of memory
These details emerge from melting snow:
Houses, roads, the likeness of a man
Dwindling, watching, coals for eyes.

Old father midnight of memory
Who never was, never could be,
Would have said: 'Go, Leave;
This is a great place to be from'.

And the future would have been blessed
In a red glass of country wine
His hand round it, round mine,
Small hairs alive in the firelight.

How to bequeath this to my strange son,
Adrift in a future I'll never make?
Strange, for unengendered,
Unconceived & inconceivable,
Another changeling with an other's gaze.

Gaze farther, son, beguilingly askew –
Drawn to the slant of your own nose
Or noose – tending
Where no-one knows.

Like Exploding Haloes

A great shunt
Of cloud mass, heavy,
Thigh-shapely, lowering
Its weather down.

I threw back my head
For a mighty faceful
Of tart refreshment
My tongue poised ready to savour –
And nothing came.

Towards the end of that decade
Of dying Summers – after the plague
Of wasps & ladybirds – we got the message,
Tuned in to the static mist,
Gilt gone from the lager-head
Not kissed quite the same by the sun.

And Bowie limped into the grey studio
Burdened by TV eye & the breath of Berlin,
His Japanese sandal chafing his toe
Forever flexing in someone else's shoe:
Dazed from duetting with Bing
In a drift of studio snow,
Then dreaming the ominous links
Where the old crooner disappeared for good
In a sudden white-out, he begins to feel
Like death's handmaiden.

Cleaning up can be hazardous.
Is death attracted to the psychic shifts
As the mental blocks are shunted?
The old bastard seems to be drawn
To painful adjustments, to strenuous realignments.

Didn't he watch, bemused, as Marc stumbled
From the stage edge during his final intro,
Laughing self-consciously as the credits rolled
Just a week before he was felled?

'Summer is Heaven in '77'... 'Singalonga me...'
– Crooning as the shadows gather,
As the dark wreath is woven
With inscrutable cunning craft.

Twenty years, since then, of dubious Summers,
Of the air dying on us, of the lungs
Closing down, the same sounds hoarsely
Spinning around. Strike a light
And watch it wither, choked
Candle or gasping match.

You'd have a devil of a job
To ignite Lucifer himself
In this miasmal air:
Even those who burn from within
Have their dirty work cut out.

•

Another relic: the old boy in the coastal pub,
His speech impediment necessitating repetitions
Beyond embarrassment, had me know
Our village was the Athens, once, of Anglesey:
An intellectual centre of repute, plus
Home to fifty cobblers, cobbling clogs
For workers to wear down the quarried mountain
To prevent the overview... (Their futile feet
Are steaming in my head).

And, too, between the cluster
Of intimate front-room pubs,
The Indian rock maker on his candy loom –

(And did the name, long & spluttersome
As it was & is, run sheer
Through each sweet stick
His dark hand turned?)

Not to neglect the umbrella-fashioning Count
(What an aristocracy of artisans!)
Who no doubt picked his way (& vampire teeth)
Beneath an ominous canopy of spoked black
He'd lovingly handcrafted
For his own exclusive use:
Gamp cunningly rigged
To collapse around the head
Of his next pale victim.

I've drifted from weather systems
By way of flawed icons, in honour
Of the manner of their going:
Accidental, arbitrary, with a mouthful
Of fog, wet ashes in their eyes, a greyness
Corresponding to the sky.

If this seems arbitrary, if the connections
Aren't evident, let me remind you
Of the intricate Celtic knotwork
Which interweaves a life with all the action
Of maggots swarming in a carcass
As the camera speeds up
Drawing us in to the deadly
Fascination of design.

The inkwell is encircled
With the snake that eats its tail.
The ink is as black as unconsciousness.
Need I say more? I will –

The Cunt, lacking his sweet saving 'O',
Stalks these narrowing passages, haunts
These stumbling stanzas, bloodlust in his pupils,
Searching for the storyline
That squares the tightening circle.

'O,O,O,O… divine aperture, peephole
To the other side, gateway in the text,
Breathing hole in the body of the word,
Most self-contained of all the letters,
The self-devouring snake meeting himself
As if a stranger, his end in his beginning
All coming together like the poetry we recognize.

'The spinning of the word,' warns
The teacher, 'breaking free of its creator,
Bucking to random changes in the weather,
May form a meaningless vortex of the air…'
But this is the adventure language creates
In rampant evolution. It can't, nor should it,
Keep all the weather out. Just see
The fabric strain. It's the nature
Of umbrellas, turning inside out
When least expected, like
Exploding haloes.

The Old Belt

He strapped on a belt
He'd bought in adolescence,
Mildewed now & straining,
And frolicked naked in it
As one who would run at things
And embrace them heedlessly
Like that girl, descending
The hill.

If he's over it, why is he labouring
Ever upwards? Chronology's curse
Turns the saw upon its head,
And the woman too, blinded by her own frills,
Kicking blunt boots at the sky
As his teeth divide her.

Cherished difference fails to convince:
What once was spice, was *frisson*,
Is now a girlish lad, thumbs hooked
In pockets, talking non-scents.

O to be blissed in that faded bower
Where finger fondles the wrinkling petal
And curls in anointments of pollen.

He could jump at the chance
In his pants, buckled beneath
An old belt.

Slow Dissolve

No-one asked how it felt
Through the layers of silence,
So I wasn't forced to translate
The thing into feeling. It meant
Nothing to me; absolutely; it was everything
Gathered into itself, a column
Of compacted print, so tight
It becomes solid in its meaning-
Lessness.

•

Just me & me, & then the world.
Nothing for or against: transferring
My image from backdrop to backdrop,
Becoming my own transparency.

Sensitive? – As unexposed film,
Tightly wound in the dark;
Prickly? – As pregnant emulsion,
Bubbling on these greenhouse afternoons.

In this glasshouse world I stalk
A storm's about to break.

•

The more of myself I become
The less I'm with you. I melt
The human containment
We once were. I blur
The relationship into the image
Of a cunt with no sides:
Just space, thrashing.

Lost Beast

What was this beast, this ancient
Animal I squirmed within
Forcing myself out through horse-hair,
Bristle, rippling pelt & hide,
Snorting the spittle of fields?

My instinct for secrecy alone remains
Of that old beauty. It's ridden down
A rough road in worn shoes,
A parallel shadow drovers' road
Where ghosts of old work & worth
Move with phantom purpose between places
Which once were destinations, haunts of destiny,
But now hang fire for lack of oxygen.

Fond nostalgia, this concept of a place
Being worthy of tryst, belonging,
Fealty, fortune, fate. Would that I
Had ever inhabited such.

From a distance, across field, across plain
You may see my nostrils flare
Miming instinctive insuck
Funnelling all the sweet surround.

The Movement You Need

Big trip, the transference of the books
From the bedside table to the writing desk.
I'd been enjoying the horizontal for a space,
A double space, getting above myself,
Floating free of the line.

So it became like shift from sick-room to the real world
And this adept at plumbing the depths
Pondered, like a pebble in the sea, engulfment,
And how it related to love, down there,
Where the visibility is minimal:
Deciding, maybe – *I love the world,*
And this includes your left shoulder
And your face above me in the forest
And my resting on your almost bare breast.

The word 'almost', perhaps, I love most of all,
And nurture as I rise & fall.

Note: the lines in italics are from
a Kafka letter to Milena

The Undeadness Of The Situation Fascinates

'How amazing to find you here!' I cry
To my doppel-toper, miraculously spinning
Out the habits of a lifetime
At a white table on the far side
Of the garden.

'*What is time but a variety of one thing?*'*
– And the setting hums perennially
As the gold falls in the glass
As the weather draws its layers across the scene
Which shifts as the sitter adjusts
His sweetening aches.

* Austin Osman Spare

Our Old & Always Love

As if at the start of a great journey,
A great adventure, turned & said:
'And where will you sleep tonight?
'With who? With who?' – 'With you'
Comes the answer, barefoot, bed-bound, soft
Across the years, as the great journey
Narrows down to dark.